Lemonada..

Langostino..

& The Universal..

Brie King?

Short Essays On

LEMONS,
LANGSTON,
& THE UNIVERSE BREAKING

by

Peter Karam

PORT TOWNSEND
PUBLISHING

Published by Port Townsend Publishing
PO Box 539 Port Townsend, Washington 98368

Made in the United States of America

The Papa-Tango logo is a trademark of
Port Townsend Publishing

www.porttownsendpublishing.com

Cover photo by Peter Karam

ISBN 978-1-964904-00-9

for people who like random essays

TABLE OF CONTENTS

LEMONS & SUGAR-WATER

Crisp, cool, clean, heavy sheets were the first feelings on my skin when I would awaken to the cooing of mourning doves through the ajar windows and the smell of bacon frying in the twilight hours of summer mornings visiting my grandparents as a child. Dew on the grass in the backyard, the chilly early a.m. quiet gently accentuated by the doves. My father and grandfather would already be up finishing the paper over some oatmeal that my grandfather always made, with fresh fruit and a cup of coffee, before I even knew it was a new day yet. By the time I was compelled to the kitchen by the smell of sizzling swine my grandfather would be outside working in the garden or tinkering on a project in the garage and if my father wasn't out helping his dad it was only to help set the table for the wonderful breakfast my grandmother had prepared, of which we would all soon be partaking. The overall attitude: work hard, but enjoy life.

After breakfast my dad and I would clean up the kitchen and my grandmother would start to tend to her flowers. Much of her gardening hours were spent on the two beautiful rows of big, healthy rose bushes that ran the length of the raised front yard. At the foot of the roses was Trailing Rosemary, oozing over the edge of the yard and down the retaining wall, perpetually covered it seemed, in delicate little powder-blue flowers and humming honeybees. The colorful and sweet-smelling roses separated the retaining-wall drop-off to the sidewalk from the lush green of the almost unbelievably thick (perhaps zoysiagrass) front lawn. The only thing that broke the plane of that soft bed of green was a big, healthy magnolia tree, perfect for a boy to climb, way up to the top even, to see over the tops of the other old one-story houses still on the street. My grandparents had built that house, on that spot, in 1938, the year following my dad's birth (youngest of three), and the year prior to the start of the Second World War, but though eighty years had lapsed, the condition of every single thing was pristine and in its own specially organized place, resultant of their constant care and upkeep. At the time that they built it, theirs was one of very few homes yet built on that quiet Santa Monica street, between the beautifully treed San Vicente Boulevard and unassuming Georgina Avenue. The huge southeast-African-native Coast Coral

Trees that wonderfully cleave in twain the northbound from the southbound lanes of San Vicente are also quite wonderful for a kid to climb, it must not be overlooked.

The bright orb of southern California sunbeams would slowly creep from one side of the private backyard to the other until it was fully engulfed in yellow warmth. The fuzzy buzzy bees would start the days work of sipping sweet-scented citrus nectar from the well-tended lemon tree and all the colorful flowers that edged the thick green grass. Hummingbirds would start zipping here and there and soon there would be a small orchestra of flittering, twittering, tweeting, buzzing and singing.

My dad and I would ourselves work in the garden or on such projects that might prove unappealing to eighty-something-year-olds. Not that they weren't fit till the very end: they surely were. They golfed into their nineties. They gardened every day, outside every day, active every day, not just physically but mentally as well, playing card games and doing crossword puzzles. My grandfather lived till he was ninety-nine, my grandmother one hundred and three, and till the end they were both moving and active and intelligent. But let's say there's a bougainvillea that thinks itself to be the giant kraken-like squid from *20,000 Leagues Under the Sea* and it's enveloping and engulfing the attached garage like its last meal. Dad and I would be on the roof of the garage and house, fighting against the long-tentacled demon, hacking it down to size and chasing it back to it's allotted domain.

This is the sort of work my dad and I love: outside. That is why as a child it seemed to me like no matter how much he scrubbed his large hands with strong soaps, washcloths, and brushes, the infinite hairline cracks on the surface of his calloused appendages seemed to be forever dark. Forever the color of the dark healthy soil he is always digging, mulching, composting, and planting in. Forever the color of the dark oil and grease and grime from long days of hauling big, heavy loads of steel or other oddity, with his flatbed 18-wheeler, when the long southern California droughts would make the dark healthy-smelling earth dry and parched for want of water. With features resembling his ancestral great-great-uncle Ulysses Simpson Grant but with a sun-darkened skin tone hinting at his bit of Indigenous American heritage or perhaps from the hint of African in his DNA, this working man enjoys a cold beer every afternoon after his long hard day's labors. The Working Man. The Batchelor's Degree from U.C. Berkeley's business school led to a suit and tie and desk and office and selling government aerospace contracts to the highest bidders around the Southwest region and becoming "a cog in the machine of war", as he put it. When that epiphany came, the suit and tie and desk and office became a speck in the rear-view mirror. That's not to say that he shirked work at all. Much the opposite in fact: the one thing I know he's proud of (not that he'd admit it easily, being fairly humble) is his work ethic: he is a hard-worker. When water was aplenty in California, he would professionally garden and landscape. When a drought would come he would drive tractor-trailer combinations; semis; 18-wheelers; big-rigs; trucks. No suit, tie, desk, office, nor cog in the machine of war.

Days of working around his folks' garden with my dad would lead to afternoons in the sun, taking breaks from cooling in a kiddy pool to sip my grandmother's best-in-the-world fresh-squeezed lemonade she had just made from the big, fat, beautifully-juicy Meyer lemons that would weigh down the old lemon tree's branches. She and I would sit in the shade, listing to birds, sipping lemonade, and play checkers or cards - gin rummy, sounds of a Dodgers' game being called on the radio by it's iconic voice Vin Scully drifting out from the house, where my grandfather would be taking a break from gardening and my father would be looking for that cool-on-the-sweaty-brow afternoon beer. Backyard Utopia.

Now that my dad himself is into the eighty-somethings, one would think he would show signs of aging. This is not the case. Now that he's "retired," all day, every day, he works around his wife's plant nursery, building shade-houses or work-sheds, or loading, hauling, and delivering dozens of heavy, potted plants all over California. When he's not doing that he's either working on a small 20-foot sailboat he put together, taking his dog for a walk, going to a pilates or yoga class, or off on a ten-mile bike ride through the foothills of the Ojai Valley. He also tends to eat fairly healthy, and all the daily activity more than makes up for the couple of afternoon beers. Which leads me to my hypothesis on living a long life (fate not withstanding):

Stay active: mentally and physically. Always work hard, but enjoy life.

And as my dad's mom, my grandmother, said until she was One-Hundred-and-Three:

Accentuate The Positive.

BEHIND "UN-AMERICAN INVESTIGATORS"

James Langston Hughes shared his infancy with the infancy of the 1900s. The main body of his work reflects the oppression he, and everyone of color, experienced under a system controlled by a majority of ignorant, racist bigots. His work voices the pain and hardship endured by the oppressed, as well as optimism towards solutions of these problems, and hope for a future not so darkly overshadowed by greed, corruption, and cruelty. Most of these works were, and still are, thought-provoking and controversial. The more controversial works even brought so much political attention to Hughes that he was called to testify before a senate subcommittee. The unkind and utterly distasteful manner in which many people were treated by this pompous and unprofessional subcommittee undoubtedly led to his 1953 poem "Un-American Investigators."

On March 24th, 1953, an executive session of the U. S. Senate was convened. The Permanent Subcommittee on Investigations of the Committee on Government Operations held hearings to determine, among other things, whether or not certain works by various writers would be allowed in libraries outside the United States. The U. S. federal government had allocated about 21 million dollars on American literature for libraries around the world for the purpose of "propagandizing the free world, the free system … the American system" as Senator Everett Dirksen of Illinois put it. Now they were investigating whether or not the works of literature in question represented the brand of Americanism they had intended to propagate in the world or if they portrayed more of a Communist message. The "Communist Threat" was the primary focus of the American government at that time and these hearings (and their hunt for "Un-American Activities") are commonly referred to as the "McCarthy Hearings" for Senator Joseph McCarthy of Wisconsin, Chairman of both the primary committee and subsequent subcommittee. They are now an infamous identifier of the social blacklisting and prejudice that can be nurtured and encouraged by the government, as it was at that time.

Mr. Hughes was brought to testify at more than one of these hearings. At the March 24th session, without transcribing the entire testimony here, it shall suffice to say that the subcommittee was rude and condescending to Hughes. Poem upon poem of Hughes' was scrutinized and criticized by the members, all with the claim that every word of every poem was Hughes' direct philosophies and beliefs. (I shall refrain from an in-depth tangent on the parallels to some modern hip-hop/rap poets and the modern courts claiming identical beliefs to those held by the 1953 subcommittee.) What no committee member (nor modern court) could seem to grasp, despite Hughes' repeated attempts to clarify these realities, are what any primary school child knows: first, some poems are written from the point of view of a character, just like with other forms of storytelling, and secondly, literature is interpreted differently by every individual who reads it. As Hughes himself responded to questions about one of his poems: "the Bible, for example, means many things to different people. That poem would mean many things to different people." Later, Hughes was questioned by Senator Dickson about another poem. The white man starts off by insinuating he himself is perhaps more in touch with the Black community than Mr. Hughes, a man of color:

> May I say, sir, from my familiarity with the Negro people for a long time that they are innately a very devout and religious people —this is the first paragraph of the poem:
> "Listen, Christ,
> You did all right in your day, I reckon—
> But that day's gone now.

They ghosted you up a swell story too,
Called it the Bible—
But it's dead now.
The popes and the preachers've
Made too much money from it.
They've sold you to too many."
Do you think that Book is dead?

Mr. Hughes: No, sir, I do not. That poem, like that handbill, is an ironical and satirical poem.

Senator Dirksen: It was not so accepted, I fancy, by the American people.

Mr. Hughes: It was accepted by a large portion of them and some ministers and bishops understood the poem and defended it.

Senator Dirksen: I know many who accepted the words for what they seem to convey.

Mr. Hughes: That is exactly what I meant to say in answer to the other gentleman's question, that poetry may mean many things to many people.

If the senators had any clue, that would have been a triumphant mic-drop for the poet, and everyone could've gone home. Instead, the senator continued on and finally asked Hughes how he thought the average reader would interpret the poem. Hughes responded:

> They are very likely often not to understand it, sir. I have found it very difficult myself to understand a great many poems that one had to study in school. If you will permit me, I will explain that poem to you from my viewpoint.

The senator basically ignored Hughes' offer and continued on his rant:

> Of course, when all is said and done a poem like this must necessarily speak for itself, because notwithstanding what may have been in your mind, what inhibitions, whether you crossed your fingers on some of those words when you wrote them, its impact on the thinking of the people is finally what counts.[1]

There thus can seem to be no question as to the inspiration for "Un-American Investigators" when we read such lines from it as:

---

[1] United States. Eighty-Third Congress, First Session. <u>Executive Sessions of the Senate Permanent Subcommittee on Investigations of the Committee on Government Operations.</u> Vol. 2, March 24, 1953.

The committee's fat,
Smug, almost secure
Co-religionists
Shiver with delight
In warm manure… (lines 1-5)

And though Hughes is of course correct that a poem can be interpreted in a myriad of ways by many different people, and it could be said that one can never be certain of a writer's inspiration or a poem's absolute meaning, here at least it seems is Hughes belief exemplified that "poetry should be direct, comprehensible, and the epitome of simplicity" as he closes it with a repeated theme:

The committee shivers
With delight in
Its manure. (lines 21-23)[2]

---

[2]Hughes, Langston. "Un-American Investigators." <u>The Compact Bedford Introduction to Literature</u>. Ed. Michael Meyer. 8th ed. Boston: Bedford/St. Martin's, 2009. 928-9.

UNIVERSAL THEOLOGIES AND FLANNERY O'CONNOR

Flannery O'Connor was born into a Catholic family and raised in the Bible Belt, the protestant South, of these United States of America. Unlike many children born into families practicing some form of religion, she not only embraced the church dogmas but seemed to deeply perceive the supernatural otherworld of spiritual enlightenment upon which all of our planet's major religions are based. She also perceived the need for a reawakening of this enlightenment in her professed religion of Catholicism. As does everything over time look more and more different from its original form, changing, degrading, decomposing just a little, day after day, so too do organized institutions, governments, businesses, churches, dogmas, religions.

The change that overcame the Christian church is so drastic it is frightening, from its origins with a handful of poor humble fishermen spreading peace and love for all people, to the pomp and arrogance so polarly opposite of that spirit, ushered in by the horrific power of organized, state-sanctioned religion. Three hundred years after Jesus is noted as saying "Love your enemies, bless them that curse you, do good to them that hate you, and pray for them which despitefully use you and persecute you"[3], the emperor Constantine reported that the Christ appeared to him in a dream, promising to vanquish his enemies, shortly before a battle which ended with Constantine's enemy's head decapitated and hoisted on the end of a pike.

Constantine followed that with organizing and empowering the Christian religion across all of the Roman world, establishing the day of sun worship as the new day of rest/worship for all, instead of the traditional Sabbath, and combining other equinox and solstice celebrations with Christian holidays, like Easter and Christmas, making it an easier institution to accept and join for the non-christians. In the same spirit of Constantine, one of his successors, Theodosius I, established the catholic orthodoxy as the national religion of the Roman Empire. This combination of church and state eventually gave the church absolute power, and as the British historian Lord Acton generally observed "absolute power corrupts absolutely."

---

[3] King James Bible. Matthew 5:44.

Thirteen hundred years after Jesus is noted as saying "Love your neighbor as yourself"[4] and "Love one another. As I have loved you, so you must love one another"[5] the Church and it's minions of sycophants and spin-off organizations were already hard at work for the Prince of Peace with the zealous torture and murder of countless innocent people, some historians estimating in the millions of dead children, women, and men over the following centuries. One such important event in the timeline of Christianity was the Catholic Revival, or Counter-Reformation, during which time some estimate that 60,000 people, predominantly women over 40, were murdered for "witchcraft". Some historians note that many of those executed were accused by their neighbors.

Thus, nearly 2,000 years after the peacenik Joshua ben Joseph (known by fans as Jesus the Christ) was preaching peace and love, breaking bread and fishes with strangers, the Catholic Church that Flannery O'Connor saw was so utterly off-course that she realized the importance of sharing the truths that had been revealed to her. She capitalized on her command of the written craft to promote her religious convictions, and used each of her stories as a magnifying glass to reinforce the reasoning behind each principle. And though O'Connor saw these beliefs as Catholic, one

---

[4] The Bible. New International Version. Mark 12:31.

[5] The Bible. New International Version. John 13:34.

could argue that they in fact reflect some basic universal theological principles.

In Webster Schott's literary critique "Flannery O'Connor: Faith's Stepchild," Schott makes the observation that "Vanity corrupts Christian belief, selfless intention, personal sacrifice," referring to the realities and characterizations in O'Connor's fiction, and accurately uses an example of the vain, yet self-professed, selfless humanitarian Mrs. Turpin from O'Connor's "Revelation" to support this. Unfortunately, though, sometimes it seems that for some readers, O'Connor's messages get lost in the boldness of the telling. Schott, for instance, seems to see no intention behind O'Connor's writing when he states that "Flannery O'Connor's work is filled with irony...But the delicious irony probably escaped her." Nor does he seem to connect with the deeper content of her work when he writes: "As patterns of thought her work suggests the absolute theological dead end."[6]

For those who do realize her Christian goals, O'Connor invites a deeper analysis. In Robert Milder's "The Protestantism of Flannery O'Connor," Milder makes the argument that O'Connor is more protestant than Catholic and uses examples from O'Connor's "Revelation" and "A Good Man is Hard to Find" (among other works) to support this: "It is so customary to speak of the 'banality of evil' that the phrase itself had become banal, yet this is precisely what Miss O'Connor

---

[6] Schott, Webster. "Flannery O'Connor: Faith's Stepchild." The Nation 201.7 (1965): 142-44, 146.

means by original sin: not the murderousness of a psychotic like the Misfit, but the complacency of Mrs. Turpin."[7]

As for the works themselves, we find that a personal lack of faith in a supreme omnipotence leads to theft and ill will in those like the false-bible-salesman in "Good Country People" when queried on his stance on Christianity and the salesman responds angrily: "'I hope you don't think,' he said in a lofty indignant tone, 'that I believe in that crap!'"[8]. He then proceeds to exact his vices towards, and to the detriment of, the non-believing atheistic Hulga, who's intent was in fact to take advantage of *him*. A personal lack of faith in a supreme omnipotence also leads to the culmination of destructiveness in the Misfit of "A Good Man is Hard to Find," whom states that if there is no deity (in this case Jesus) "'then it's nothing for you to do but enjoy the few minutes you got left the best way you can - by killing somebody or burning down his house or doing some other meanness to him. No pleasure but meanness'"[9]. We find that selfishness and egocentricity leads to not only the destruction of oneself but also to

[7] Milder, Robert. "The Protestantism of Flannery O'Connor." The Southern Review XI (1975): 802-19.

[8] O'Connor, Flannery. "Good Country People." The Compact Bedford Introduction to Literature. Ed. Michael Meyer. 8th ed. Boston: Bedford/St. Martin's, 2009. 391.

[9] O'Connor, Flannery. "A Good Man is Hard to Find." The Compact Bedford Introduction to Literature. Ed. Michael Meyer. 8th ed. Boston: Bedford/St. Martin's, 2009. 376-7.

those closest to oneself in the grandmother character of "A Good Man is Hard to Find." If she hadn't been so intent on always getting her way, the tale tells us, she would not be directly responsible for the deaths of her family and herself: she insists on detouring down a side road to find a house she's made up stories about and that she later remembers is in a different state altogether; she insists on sneaking the cat in the car, which gets loose and jumps on the driver, her son, causing them to roll the car over, leaving them stranded and at the mercy of a man she identifies as the Misfit. These self-serving, hard-headed acts lead to the final scenes, wherein her identification of him prompts the Misfit to respond: "'...it would have been better for all of you, lady, if you hadn't reckernized me,'"[10] shortly followed by the fatal gunfire that ends the entire family.

The moral principles that O'Connor uses her stories to emphasize can be seen honored in writings from all the major religions of the world. In the Hindu Bhagavad-Gita or The Song of God as translated by Swami Prabhavananda and Christopher Isherwood, God, incarnated in the form of Sri Krishna, gives direction that is reflective of the messages of O'Connor: "Control the lusts of your heart, and renounce the fruits of every action. Concentration [on God] which is practiced with discernment is certainly

---

[10] O'Connor, Flannery. "A Good Man is Hard to Find." The Compact Bedford Introduction to Literature. Ed. Michael Meyer. 8th ed. Boston: Bedford/St. Martin's, 2009. 373.

better than the mechanical repetition of a ritual or a prayer. Absorption in God –to live with Him and be one with Him always– is even better than concentration. But renunciation [of worldly attachments: lust, desires, etc] brings instant peace to the spirit. A man should not hate any living creature. Let him be friendly and compassionate to all"[11]

In the Tao Te Ching, or here as The Way of Life According to Lao Tzu, translated by Witter Bynner, the enlightened sage bestows similar wisdom: "Be utterly humble and you shall hold to the foundation of peace. Be at one with all these living things" and "Before creation a presence existed, self-contained, complete, formless, voiceless, mateless, changeless, which yet pervaded itself with unending motherhood. Though there can be no name for it, I have called it 'the way of life'"[12]. So there also, though Lao Tzu doesn't go so far as to define a clear deity, per se, his message is for all to come into union with an everlasting omnipotence that has existed since "before creation".

In M. H. Shakir's translation of The Qur'an we read that "whoever submits himself entirely to Allah and he is the doer of good (to others) he has his reward from his Lord, and there is no fear for him nor shall he

---

[11] The Song of God: Bhagavad-Gita. Trans. Swami Prabhavananda & Christopher Isherwood. England: Phoenix House Ltd., 1972. 98-9.

[12] The Way of Life According to Lao Tzu. Trans. Witter Bynner. New York: Capricorn Books, 1962. 33-4, 40.

grieve"[13]. Each of these precepts, and others like them, are the driving theme's in O'Connor's work: as Mrs. Turpin sees in a vision in "Revelation," the grandmother's epiphany in "A Good Man is Hard to Find" and Helga's motives and actions being turned back onto her in "Good Country People," we are none better than another and selfishness leads to nowhere beneficial.

Therefore, it is arguably conclusive that if we not only just use the Catholic lens, as O'Connor directs, or even the Protestant lens, as Milder suggests, but an even broader theological lens to absorb her messages through, with unbiased imaginations we could undoubtedly draw the same ideal theological conclusions as was the gist and spirit of her intentions: without faith in something bigger than ourselves there is no point to anything, no perfection for which to aspire, nothing to measure good and bad against —no accountability, thus no hope for humanity; without faith/trust/conviction/belief of something deeper and larger than the fumbling frailty of our petty grey matter and its mortal encasement, chaos reigns.

---

[13] The Qur'an. Trans. M.H. Shakir. New York: Tahrike Tahsile Qur'an, Inc., 2002. 10.

AN OUTSIDER'S TAKE ON STRAIGHT'S "MINES"

Susan Straight was born in 1961 and has lived all of her life, at least so far as to the point of this writing, in Southern California. Her relationships with friends and family, both incarcerates and corrections officers, gave her a very real and solid background for bringing to life her 2002 short story "Mines." This short story hits on current social issues that are so much day-to-day life that they are for the most part overlooked by the general American populace. It is a story about a community and the cultures within that community, as told by the main character, Clarette, a corrections officer and mother. Through Clarette's eyes we come to behold a number of key points. Firstly, we are faced with grand-scale problematic cultural patterns that perhaps have no easy answers, if they have solutions as all. Secondly, and separately, is the delicate balance between work and home-life that we all must negotiate. And ultimately, that all these issues interconnect.

On the problematic patterns theme, the collection of cyclical cultural issues is really a bottomless pit of topics and discussion, but for this particular analysis focus will be mainly concentrated upon the tragic inner-city male youth mentality that many young men of color especially feel is their only defense in a world out to get them: "'…them little boys, they go off to the prison just like the army. Like they have to. To be a man'"[14]. As Clarette describes the youth in her correctional facility: shaved heads and tattoos, organized and self-segregated by nationality, we are painted a very real portrait, because all these characterizations ring true-to-life to anyone who themselves or who's friends or relatives have had to spend any amount of time on the other side of the bars in our nation's correctional institutions. The general mentality of these incarcerated youth *does* seem to be as quoted above, per the characterizations in the story and from personal societal observations and interactions. The young inmates in the story mirror their counterparts in the real world and glorify their 'thug-

---

[14] Straight, Susan. "Mines." <u>The Compact Bedford Introduction to Literature</u>. Ed. Michael Meyer. 8th ed. Boston: Bedford/St. Martin's, 2009. p158.

life' so much as to even joke about going to the adult correctional facility across the street from theirs.

Our everyday every-woman heroine Clarette is not only faced with thug-life appeal in the faces and interactions of those she is paid to herd, but on the home-front as well. Her son's father encourages this mentality, which is a challenge to Clarette. As when the father, Ray, has the son's head shaved, and to her rebuke the father responds: "Like Mike, baby. Like Ice Cube. The look." During the time in which this story is set, Ice Cube was not as family-friendly as he sometimes chooses to be these days. Cube first gained international attention as a member of the pioneering gangsta-rap group N.W.A., which does not stand for Nonconformists With Angst, but could have, had they been born into a more privileged place in society. But, since our current societies and institutions have historically been organized in a manner with which to suppress people of color, N.W.A. became famous and controversial for such songs as "Fuck tha Police" and Cube himself for solo hits like "I Wanna Kill Sam" (as in 'Uncle Sam'). Thus Clarette's frustration that this is the role-model that not only her son's father has chosen to raise their boy up to, but that a large percent of her social sub-culture has accepted the same: "Oh, yeah. He looks like Ice Cube, nobody's gonna mess with him. All better, right? Damn you, Ray"[15].

On the other side she is antagonized by a self-righteous egotist: "'Doesn't it hurt your soul? How can

---

[15] p157-8.

you stand it?'"[16], "'How can you work at the youth prison? All those young brothers incarcerated by the system?' … 'Doesn't it hurt you to be there?'"[17]. The antagonist seems to almost be blaming Clarette for being involved in some large, race-driven conspiracy, insinuating there were only young black men locked up, when from Clarette's point of view all nationalities are represented: "All the damn heads look the same to me…Chicano kids and the Vietnamese…Filipino…the white kids…"[18]. In direct contrast, her antagonist presses on: "'Prison is the biggest growth industry in California. They're determined to put everyone of color behind a wall'"[19]. On seemingly every side Clarette is confronted by the mentality that the "young brothers" locked up had no choice, option or decision on the path to their incarceration. As these scenes ring true, so too do the frustrated concerns of those on both sides of these issues. Although Clarette may have differing opinions on the topic, her time is not so easily spent theorizing on these issues on the large scale; she's just trying to be a productive member of her community and society by raising her children up to be the same, how she sees is right, and just living life day to day: "… Danae's got asthma. I don't get to worry about big stuff like you do, cause I'm worrying about big stuff like I do.

[16] p154.

[17] p153.

[18] p155.

[19] p155.

Pay the bills, put gas in the van, buy groceries"[20]. At another point she is almost accused by some woman at the hair-dressers of locking up the woman's son: "Shouldn't be mad at me. 'I didn't got her son. I'm just tryin to make sure he comes home…'"[21].

Clarette's stresses at home bleed over into work, both indirectly: "'Shut the fuck up, Fred.' … I hear it come out like that, and I close my eyes"[22] and directly, in that one of the inmates she is charged with maintaining is her little nephew. Her stresses at work, in turn, bleed over into home life: "'Why you yelling, Mama? I see how to do it.' …He grinned. I wanted to cry"[23]; "…When I get home now, and the kids start their homework, I have to stand at the sink and wash my hands and change my mouth. My spit, everything, I think"[24]. Thus Clarette is faced with the challenges faced by all: parental/familial duty above everything and the search for place and purpose in this world.

Not much can be said about the specific examples of resolution found by the end of the story without giving it all away, but suffice it to say that some definite resolution is reached, by the strength and resolve of the narrator, our hero, Clarette. And although all the

---

[20] p154.

[21] p159.

[22] p154.

[23] p158.

[24] p154.

stress is consistent and never-ending, Ms. Straight shows us that it is how we handle this over-lapping of the alternate realities of work and home that is important. It is displayed that only by balancing the home life can social change be accomplished and breaking out of cultural stereotypic roles takes acts outside of culture-specific norms, but is ultimately necessary to achieve growth.

WHERE DID THE TIMBER GO?

Boise Cascade, Georgia-Pacific, ITT Rayonier, Weyerhaeuser and other such corporations began exporting raw logs from *industrially* clear-cut Pacific Northwest (PNW) National Forests by at least the early 1960s. Upwards of 80 billion board feet (bf) of raw logs were exported between the early 1960s and the mid 1990s. The 1990s saw, on average, 2+ billion bf of raw logs exported *per year* from the West Coast (Oregon and Washington being the primary contributor to that amount) not including wood chips or other such processed materials. Northwest wood chips exported in an average year neared 3 billion bf. This means that in the 1990s the northwest exported about 45% of its harvest.

Despite its "abundant domestic forest resources"[25] Japan has remained the number one destination for raw U.S. northwest logs since World War II up until fairly recently. And it wasn't number one by a slim margin either, with NW log exports to Japan peaking in 1989 with 2.4 billion board feet. Various factors in Japan, including rising costs of transportation, road construction, timber harvesting and logging wages, compared against Japan's economical and efficient coastal milling industry, resulted in the fact that importing raw logs from the U.S. PNW was just plain cheaper than harvesting local Japanese timber. Despite Japan paying a comparatively high price for quality PNW old growth logs, their cheap labor combined with their ability to recover about 20% more product from the logs than U.S. mills could, more than made up for the higher price, overseas shipping, and import costs. This continued for about three decades and has only recently seen a shift (only 706,000 bf from the PNW to Japan at the end of the 20th century, year 2000) owing to the harvestable maturity of forests that the Japanese mass-replanted after W.W.II.

More recent northwest timber harvests for Oregon and Washington gleaned nearly six billion bf in 2010 (roughly 3 billion from each state). A very small percent (<9%) was from public lands managed by the Bureau of Land Management (BLM). Instead it came from mostly

_____

25 Daniels, J.M. U.S. Department of Agriculture, Forest Service. (2005). *The rise and fall of the pacific northwest log export market* (PNW-GTR-624).

state public lands and private properties. Nearly 19% of the harvest (just over 1 billion bf) was exported, a 59% increase in timber harvesting, made possible by joint ventures between the timber corporations and congressional leaders, in order to fulfill China's want of wood. China, exampling how it is possible to go into ecological debt, over-harvested their forests and are now eagerly buying in the U.S. Pacific Northwest. The export to China in 2010 was 495 million bf, or $306 million of the $697 million dollars of northwest forests sent overseas as raw logs.

China is also purchasing vast amounts of timber from Russia and Canada as well, but those nations have forward-thinking log export tariff laws in place in order to protect their environmental capital from being given away wholesale to other nations. So, unlike the less expensive, bulk shipments of raw logs they get from the U.S., China is forced to purchase pricier, finished lumber from those more protective nations. Prior to these tariff laws and their nation's vast deforestation, China, in 2001, imported from Russia roughly 250,000 cubic meters (m^3) of lumber. From the U.S. and Canada it imported similar amounts. In 2010 China imported that same amount of lumber from the U.S. as it has since 2001, but it imported about 3.5 million m^3 from Canada and 3.8 million m^3 from Russia. Russia's goal of increased domestic manufacturing by completely stopping the export of logs is working. Now Russia and Canada are both "exporting nearly 15 times more finished lumber to China than they were 10 years ago, two or three times more than just two years ago"[26].

It's not that we don't have agencies or laws in place to safeguard our resources, because we most certainly do. And the northwest forests were under the microscope for a while because of the disappearing Spotted Owl. Government agencies on the federal level, especially the Forest Service and Bureau of Land Management, are both government agencies that were created by Congress and had "dual objectives of conserving natural resources for future generations and maintaining the stability of the industries and communities that depend on revenues from exploiting those resources"[27]. Thus, there are federal laws requiring both the BLM and the Forest Service to conduct their tree harvesting at a sustainable pace. But in the 1980s, agency employees, by disregarding the overarching mission of the agency, many times under great pressure from the Reagan presidential administration, acted in support of the timber industry status quo, despite scientists' research and supportive data identifying the problems this deforestation causes and providing potential solutions. Of course many other high-level political appointees, prompted by the owl/timber issue's salience with the public and industry, became involved on both sides of the argument, some

[26] Crane, J. (2011, August 11). Oregon and Washington log exports cost thousands of jobs. *The Oregonian*.

[27] Layzer, J. (2012). *The environmental case: Translating values into policy*. (3rd ed., p. 174 & 175). Washington, DC: CQ Press.

trying to ride the middle ground so as not to ruffle too many feathers and not get reelected. This greater public interest, provided in large part by the litigations brought forth by environmental groups who "can challenge the dominance of extractive interests,"[28] like the mainstream moderate environmental organizations such as Oregon Wilderness Coalition, and then also by the more extreme factions, like Earth First!, whose members presented themselves as physical barriers to the timber industry's progress, by chaining themselves to trees, among other acts. Finally the Courts acted to help ensure fairness in congressional regulation review due to the questionable policies and decisions of some congressional representatives. There was much involvement at the state government level, with state agencies and committees, like the Oregon Endangered Species Task Force. The timber-workers organized themselves into coalitions as well, like the Oregon Lands Coalition. The Clinton presidential administration passed a new Northwest Forest Plan in response to the overwhelming amount of scientific evidence pointing towards the need for a more sustainable harvest approach, but a short while later a Republican-led congress gutted much of it, and the G.W. Bush presidential administration continued down this path that ultimately benefited the large international timber corporations, while retaining very little natural resource capital domestically.

---

[28] Layzer, J. (2012). *The environmental case: Translating values into policy.* (3rd ed., p. 174 & 175). Washington, DC: CQ Press.

Over the past 20 years many factors, including environmental lawsuits and a massive drop in Japanese demand, cut timber harvests, causing local economies to plummet, and enabling socio-economic hardships to easily befall northwest rural communities. The Northwest Economic Adjustment Initiative (NWEAI) is a Federal program that was developed and implemented in order to help counties in this major timber region, which primarily includes nearly 3/4ths of Washington, the western half of Oregon, and the northeast corner of California. The program provides coordination and management of economic assistance to the region in order to help address the dropping employment rate that reflected the drop in log harvesting. But as many believe, Federal assistance is not a long-term fix (don't tell the corn industry, but that's a story for another time) and it doesn't amount to the same as higher employment would. This leads many traditional Northwest families to the conclusion that if only we could get back to those logging numbers from the 1970s and 80s the socio-economic lift would fix it all and we could all live happily ever after. But those socio-economic hardships had in fact been increasing prior to the Spotted Owl hullaballoo due to the timber industry's shift to logging the southeast and moving millwork overseas.

But why did the industry move major logging and milling out of the area? Well, those unsustainable harvest practices warned of earlier by scientists and forestry professionals had a large part to play in those industry moves. Yes, there actually are a limited number of harvestable trees that can be gleaned from one area, though some like to make believe that forests are limitless. As economist Terry Raettig and research sociologist Harriet Christensen reported in the USDA Forest Service's technical report *Timber Harvesting, Processing, and Employment in the Northwest Economic Adjustment Initiative Region: Changes and Economic Assistance*:

> "Most of the harvest from private lands in the region comes from second-growth stands. By 1994, 91 percent of the timber harvest in western Washington was considered young growth ... This lack of old-growth inventory and dependence on second-growth stands limit the ability of private owners to increase harvests to compensate for declining timber harvests from Federal lands. To the extent that private owners increase harvest from immature stands in response to increasing prices, the potential for future revenues also may be compromised"[29].

In other words we're over-harvesting just like Japan and China did, and once we've allowed our resources to be given away to competing foreign powers we'll be

[29] Christensen, H.H., & Raettig, T.L. U.S. Department of Agriculture, Forest Service. (1991). *Timber harvesting, processing, and employment in the northwest economic adjustment initiative region: Changes and economic assistance* (PNW-GTR-465).

forced to do the same thing that China is doing: importing even more high-priced lumber from Canada and Russia than we already are. Hopefully China will be good enough to continue to loan the U.S. the funds needed to do that.

And why did the timber industry move lumber milling overseas? Well, if overseas mills can purchase unmilled logs so cheaply and en-mass from the U.S. they can easily afford the shipping costs and still make quite a profit when selling us back our own trees, now milled, at a substantial price mark-up.

Research forester Jean Daniels, in the 2005 USDA's Forest Service technical report *The Rise and Fall of the Pacific Northwest Log Export Market*, observes:

> "Canada is the main competitor for the United States in Pacific Rim markets. The Pacific Rim is Canada's second largest export destination for softwood lumber (the first being the United States) with over 7 Million cubic meters shipped in 1996... Canada remains the largest exporter of lumber in the world, and the United States is the largest importer of Canadian lumber. Although the United States remains Canada's strongest competitor"[30].

---

[30] Daniels, J.M. U.S. Department of Agriculture, Forest Service. (2005). *The rise and fall of the pacific northwest log export market* (PNW-GTR-624)

So, to clarify: the U.S. is Canada's biggest competitor, but also it's biggest customer. That is like Lowe's having to buy all it's lumber from Home Depot. And confoundingly, from 1982 to 2002 U.S. softwood imports from Canada more than doubled. This returns us to the topic of export restrictions such as export tariffs as a means to increase available timber supplies to PNW and other U.S. lumber mills, resulting not only in increased competitiveness in the global lumber market, but also higher employment in a larger domestic processing industry, and potentially lower lumber prices domestically, causing other potential dominoes to fall, such as lower new-build housing costs, etc.

Unfortunately, the timber industry and other vested interests have successfully kept much of this out of the general public conversation, and instead have convinced local folks in these hard-hit communities that more logging equals more jobs and stronger families, obscuring the facts that more logging just means some international corporation can make a quick buck by selling U.S. forests to Asia for cheap. The loggers would be relatively short-term employed, and then right back in the soup line, so to speak, when our nation has no more mature trees, investors' pockets are fat, and China is building a strong nation with massive piles of our discount timber. Exporting unmilled timber without protective policies and tariffs in place simply goes against America's national interests.

Faced with the realities of a finite resource, a land-management technique that is in contrast to logging is designating land as "wilderness". This method doesn't siphon large amounts of cash into international investors pockets though, so the timber industry of course wants 'No New Wilderness!'. But new wilderness designations don't mean the loss of long-term logging jobs because, if you've been paying attention to the reports cited in this essay, the U.S. no longer has mature forests that could sustain an industry at even a fraction of the pace, volume, or quality of previous eras in the history of northwest logging, and even that for only a limited time; thus, there are no more long-term logging-related jobs in the northwest. With new lands designated 'wilderness' comes new jobs, albeit in occupations alternate to logging, but those lands too need to be managed and maintained, studied and supervised. And more wilderness brings more money and jobs related to the northwest's newest, largest, economic sector: tourism. So one could argue that the best actions we can take to strengthen our nation and it's communities is by supporting protections for our forests like high export tariffs, supporting new wildernesses, and making sure our communities have the training needed to become successful again (e.g. more efficient milling techniques - how are Japanese mills able to get 20% more lumber out of trees than our mills?).

Fortunately for northwest forests, the Elwha Dams Removal Project brought them back into the public eye a bit, helping forests regain some part of their salience within communities. Projects such as this, coupled with a rising public awareness of the fragility of our biosphere are helping bring issues such as northwest timber harvesting and exportation to the forefront of public discourse. State and Federal legislations are already in place to address many of these issues, but obviously some things need to be re-looked-at, and shortcomings in policy need to be rectified. The only way that happens is if enough determined people become involved in making those rectifications a priority. Unpartisan political achievements, where both sides compromise in the endeavor to make things better for everyone, seem like a thing of fantasy sometimes, but when faced with all accumulated knowledge, research, and data, pointing in one clear direction that we, as human society, need to move in order for our planet to continue to sustain our human lives, partisan politics looks pretty petty.

Other Helpful Sources: [31] [32] [33]

[31] Hsuan, A.(2010, February 26). Oregon, Washington wood exports to Asia improve in 2009. *The Oregonian*.

[32] Perez-Garcia, J., & Barr, J. College of Forest Resources, Northwest Environmental Forum. (2005). *Forest products export trends update for the pacific northwest region*.

[33] Warren, D.D. U.S. Department of Agriculture, Forest Service. (2011). *Production, prices, employment, and trade in northwest forest industries, all quarters 2010* (PNW-RB-260)

TEXTBOOK EXTORTION

"In a world where you can download a best-seller for $10 to $13, the price of college textbooks seems pretty egregious. It's not unusual for a hardcover full-color textbook to cost $200 or more. Surely, it's time to fight back against greedy publishers and arrogant professors indifferent to the economic plight of their students. Or…maybe it's not that simple"[34].

My father is a gardener by passion, but he also got a degree in business from U.C. Berkeley and is one of the most informed and well-read persons I know, so when his reaction to me, sharing my own surprise at how much I was to spend on books for the fall quarter, was to call it "extortion," I had to take pause. After

---

[34] Weston, Liz. "Should Textbooks Really Cost $200?" *MSN Money*. Money.msn.com, 26 Oct. 2011. Web. 05 Nov. 2011.

looking the word up in the dictionary, in order to ascertain the accuracy of my previous perception of its usage and meaning, I came to the conclusion that he was, not surprisingly, most astute in his summation of the circumstances. Two hundred dollars for my biology textbook after shipping and handling and still cheaper than the local college bookstore (enough so that even a pro go-local enthusiast can't help but order online), similar situation for the chemistry textbook, but 'only' $50 for the literature textbook and a bit less for the writer's aid. These *four* books totaled almost $500 when all was said and done, due to the fact that the newest updated versions of each book were required for every class. "Current School Textbook Manufacture and Market Practices Are Unacceptable" was my original title. The high cost and too-frequent publication of "updated" editions make it obvious that the money-making machine of college textbooks has grown out of control. There can't be that many breakthroughs in Algebra or Biology over every summer, or any long established subject really, to justify the mass deforestation and unnecessary price gouging by the profiteering print moguls.

If there are some minor additions or corrections, these could be available online or in a minor printed supplement. There's no reason that a Biology textbook that hardly differs at all from the previous edition should even be made, but for the monetary gains of relatively very few. In the early 1990s at a number of U.S. colleges and universities, and in particular at one point, Ohio State, the University of Southern California, the University of Wisconsin, Cornell and Harvard, instructors were using online textbook databases to have build-it-yourself textbooks, pulling material from the schools' hundreds of sources to tailor their courses. But that must not have taken off on a large scale because in 2004 a U.S. Congressional House subcommittee searched for answers to why college textbooks cost so much. Cited report findings indicated that students at four-year educational institutions paid approximately $900 per year for textbooks and two-year institution students about $800. According to the National Center for Education Statistics, $800 a year was about 40% of the average tuition per year at a two-year school, $1,900. David Zhou, in his 2005 article in the *Christian Science Monitor* "College Textbook Prices Are Unfair and Unnecessary: [ALL Edition]," argues that the exorbitant cost "would be easier to accept if textbooks simply cost that much to manufacture. However, publishers routinely sell identical copies overseas for only a fraction of the US price. Last year, my friend bought for $60 an "international edition" math book the identical American twin of which sells for over $100 more. Even in England in recent years, the prices for identical books have been half those in the US"[35].

So who exactly is profiting? Is it the printers? The timber industry? Publishers? Bookstores? The writers?

---

[35] Zhou, David. "College Textbook Prices Are Unfair and Unnecessary: [ALL Edition]." *The Christian Science Monitor*, 19 Sept. 2005: 09.

Peggy Orchowski brings that answer to light in "Congress Questions Sky-high Costs of College Textbooks":

> According to a study of book costs at California universities and community colleges by the California Student Public Interest Research Group (CALPIRG), textbook publishers are driving up book costs.
>
> The group's director, Merriah Fairchild, said their study, "Ripoff 101: How the Current Practices of the Publishing Industry Drive Up the Cost of College Textbooks," found that "textbook publishers often produced new editions with few significant content changes, rendering older, used versions of the book obsolete and unavailable. (The publishers use gimmicks, bells and whistles such as CD-ROMs and workbooks that 64 percent of faculty surveyed said they use 'rarely' or 'never' and which artificially inflate the cost of the textbooks."[36]

In 2007 Harvard, Claremont-McKenna and a number of other prestigious colleges started using, as one writer put it "a well-regarded open-source"

---

[36] Orchowski, Peggy. "Congress Questions Sky-high Costs of College Textbooks." *Black Issues In Higher Education*. 21.14 (2004).

economics textbook written by a California Institute of Technology economics professor, R. Preston McAfee, who "gave it away - online"[37]. His reasoning: "I couldn't continue assigning idiotic books that are starting to break \$200." Some universities and colleges have placed much of their curricula online, such as the famous MIT, Massachusetts Institute of Technology, including nearly a couple thousand courses, exams, problems and video lectures. The California Community Colleges Board of Governors showed support for open educational resources, facilitating the Foothill-De Anza Community College District, in the Silicon Valley area, and other two-year colleges to encourage the creation and use of digital textbooks. But at U.C. Berkeley a researcher at the university's Center for Studies in Higher Education, Diane Harley, doubted that professors would "embrace digital course materials unless they were high quality and tailored to their often unique scholarship"[38]. Fortunately it has been proven since the early 1990s that quality and unique tailoring are already one of the main selling points of digital texts. According to Byron W. Brown, a professor of economics at Michigan State University, in an article for *The New York Times*, "Because an e-text has no resale value, it is a near perfect solution to the publishers' marketing problem [of unnecessary, costly

---

[37] Holland, Gale. "Reformers Target High Price of College Texts." *Los Angeles Times*, 20 Aug. 2008.

[38] Holland, Gale. "Reformers Target High Price of College Texts." *Los Angeles Times*, 20 Aug. 2008.

new physical books] … And their pricing of the e-text, at $79.49, approximately twice the students' net price in the used [physical book] market, assures that the money pipeline will continue to flow"[39]. Consoling news for those who were concerned that a more widespread use of used textbooks might poke a hole in publishers' overstuffed pockets.

Who decides what editions are used each term? The school or the teacher or the state or who? At some colleges it depends on the department: sometimes teachers have a say in what textbook they use, but more often than not it's the administrators who decide, not the teachers. In 2010 a new federal regulation targeted at textbook pricing went into effect. It mandated that publishers' representatives actually tell college faculty members the cost of the textbooks they were trying to pitch. It also dictated publishers "unbundle" materials such as CDs and workbooks from the textbooks, allowing them to be bought separately, in an attempt to somewhat cut the overall unnecessary costs to students. It didn't. The proof is in the pocketbook; see paragraph two of this essay; textbooks are still well over $200 each.

Students and teachers all over the nation are speaking out, finding the greater common voice amongst us and demanding some accountability and some changes, as are even some of our state and federal representatives. Actual change takes time, but

---

[39] Brown, Byron. "The Faux Value of E-Textbooks." *The New York Times*, 29 Jul. 2010.

it's coming. Washington State's community-college board is using $750,000 of state funds, matched by $750,000 from the Bill & Melinda Gates Foundation, to create low-cost textbooks and course materials to be distributed online. The online digital open-source library is "free and available to anyone who wants to use it"[40].

But for now my friend next to me in Biology paid over $200 for the 9th edition of the text (required for the class), as did I. But I also bought the previous (8th) edition online from a student in Oregon for about $30. Buying used textbooks is an adequate solution. According to Professor Byron Brown, "by buying used, and then reselling, a student can drive that cost down to $41.10"[41]. After comparing the two editions of my Biology books I found no major differences other than a larger introduction in the newer one. I returned the newer edition and was at no loss in the class. From my local college bookstore I rented the 'outdated' edition of the required Chemistry book for approximately $25 for the entire year, less than it would cost to even buy the older edition, and obviously about $200 cheaper than the "required" newer edition. When comparing these two editions, along with comparing other courses' textbooks, I again and again found no

---

[40] Long, Katherine. "Low-cost Textbooks for College Students Make Debut." *Seattle Times*, 31 Oct. 2011.

[41] Brown, Byron. "The Faux Value of E-Textbooks." *The New York Times*, 29 Jul. 2010.

significant differences between editions, usually mainly just larger introductions.

There are steps students and faculty can take to mitigate the outrageous cost of college textbooks, from small to large actions. By simply shopping around, buying used texts, students speaking with faculty about the need (or not) for the newest editions, professors addressing the topic with their department heads, administrators not willing to pad the pockets of the textbook reps and publishers, or by taking it on full-steam and starting a local campaign to address the issue, anyone with any level of desired participation can fight for themselves against textbook extortion. Those with a will to "fight back against greedy publishers" or just a desire for a reasonably priced textbook can uncover worlds of information and resources at maketextbooksaffordable.org.

Can we say "Occupy Textbooks" everyone?

Other Helpful Sources: [42] [43]

---

[42] "Computer-tailored Texts Make Imprint on College Campuses." *Marketing News* 27.21 (1993): 6.

[43] The New York Times Editorial Board (The Board). "That Textbook Costs How Much? $200?" *NYTimes: The Board*, 10 Apr. 2008.

THE AGED BARD OF AVON

"That hand shall burn in never-quenching fire that staggers thus my person"[44] is my favorite way to say "Oww quit-it; no touching." There is an endless sea of classic quotables from the expansive myriad of William Shakespeare's writings, including that gem from *Richard II*. Though many people know lines from his plays like "a rose by any other name..."[45] or "Et tu, Brute?"[46] because they are so much a part of modern culture and speech that many folks may not even realize these lines are from Shakespeare. And the amount of people is even fewer who completely

---

[44] *Richard II;* act 5, scene 5, lines 111-2.

[45] *Romeo and Juliet;* act 2, scene 2.

[46] *Julius Caesar;* act 3, scene 1.

comprehend the content of most of the actual text and therefore get to completely appreciate the wit, the candor, the romance, the simplicities and complexities that lie therein. So broadly not understood is Shakespeare, in fact, that it becomes a task, a painful chore that is only faced when forced by an English or poetry professor in school. So aside from taking someone's word for it, a person wouldn't be able to know that Shakespeare was, in fact, a great storyteller. Then one could even easily argue that Shakespeare is out-dated. *Who even really understands Old English these days anyway?* But this need not be the case. With patience and perseverance, one can come to their own personal realization that Shakespeare's works are timeless.

Unless someone "has not so much brain as ear-wax"[47], with patience and perseverance most goals can be obtainable. If one's goal is to understand what in the heck they were trying to say in all those Shakespeare plays, then a better familiarity and comprehension of Old English would be a good avenue to start down. Probably the most engaging route for a Shakespearean novice to begin with these days would be modern film adaptations. The most youthful, original, and captivating would arguably have to be Baz Luhrmann's 1996 *Romeo + Juliet*, staring Leonardo DiCaprio and Claire Danes in the title roles. And whereas the scenes and settings are visually contemporary, Luhrmann stays fairly true to the original Old English so as not to lose

---

[47] *Troilus and Cressida;* act 5, scene 1, line 49.

the genius that is Shakespeare's writing. Another acclaimed modern director, screen-writer, actor, and a student of Shakespearean theater that makes the old masterworks better understood is Kenneth Branagh. As an actor, Branagh obviously completely understands and loves Shakespearean text, but he also pauses and inflects in just the right places so as to make the old language more comprehendible to modern English-speakers. Even Americans :) . As a director he seems to make sure everyone else in the film, too, understands and feels what they are portraying. This is seen in all his films, including his visually delightful, star-studded, and *only* full-length version of *Hamlet* in film to date.

After a "wannabe Shakespeare appreciator"[48] (as a mentor put it) had whetted their appetite with the modern film and theater interpretations and started to acclimate to the old-style sentence structure and word usage, the final breakthrough might not come until many a play was read. And re-read. It is said the best way to learn a new (or in this case *old*) language or dialect is immersion. Perhaps the easiest way would be to find a favorite Shakespeare film, become familiar with it (watch it until you understand what they are saying) and then read the play. The more plays one reads, the greater the understanding and, undoubtedly, deeper the appreciation will be. But perhaps our wannabe Shakespeare appreciator is discouraged by the misperception that all Shakespeare is tragic or a love story. This is not the case. He wrote

---

[48] Goshen, Kate.

something for everyone. These *do* include romances, sonnets and poems, though many of the most famous today are the tragedies the likes of *Romeo and Juliet, Othello, Julius Caesar, Hamlet, Macbeth* and *King Lear*. But there are as many equally famous comedies, such as Love's Labour's Lost, A Midsummer-Night's Dream, Much Ado About Nothing, and As You Like It (each with great movie adaptations by the way), as there are histories, the gamut of which are many times overlooked (though they are some of my all-time favorites of Sir Bill's works). Among these histories lies the epic historical saga of the "war of the roses": the multigenerational family feud between relatives descended from the same throne of England, spreading across the Isles and France. In chronological order, it begins with *The Tragedy of King Richard II*, followed by *King Henry IV* parts One and Two, *The Life of King Henry V*, *King Henry VI* parts One, Two, and Three, and ending with *The Tragedy of King Richard III*.

Okay, admittedly, no great Shakespearean play is devoid of any major theme altogether. As in, the histories and tragedies and comedies all have their share of romance to some extent, just as each play has its share of adventure and irony and twisted realism. And Shakespearean comedies are not devoid of some form of tragedy because they are not devoid of life; they have a depth that can only be attained by the study of the real. Truth *is* stranger than fiction. Shakespeare wrote about what he saw, heard, and read. He combined the past, present and potential

futures for his characters. He brought characters to life and put them to death.

Thinking of Shakespeare as something enjoyable and even fun perhaps seems so foreign that, by now, you're no doubt thinking "More of your conversation would infect my brain"[49] so I'll keep this last part short. As with all reading, if one wants to really absorb what is being read, distractions are the enemy. Even simply listening to music might be too much. Though some quiet orchestration in the classical genre might not hinder too greatly, like a pleasant baroque piece would perhaps be apropos. But nothing too distracting of course. Not if one really wants to discover for themselves why William Shakespeare is considered one of the best writers of all time. Now tarry a mote and I shall cease posthaste my blathering on about how awesome Shakespeare is before you "desire we may be better strangers"[50].

---

[49] *Coriolanus;* act 2, scene 1, line 86.

[50] *As You Like It;* act 3, scene 2, line 263.

THE UNIVERSE IS BREAKING

A novice theorist with a terse education in chemistry and a minor awareness of the cosmos could stumble upon the similarities between basic atomic chemistry and the workings of our solar system. When the similarities between chemistry and the universe are studied a little more and chemical theory applied to the cosmos, that aforementioned novice could conclude that the universe is breaking apart piece by piece and only time (lots of it) will prove how far the universe and all its parts will be broken down.

Solar systems could be compared to atoms with their orbiting electrons, each rotating on their own polar axis as they circle the high-density, high-energy nuclei. Galaxies then in turn could be compared to simple chemical compounds, clustered arrangements of atoms forming a larger body. The entire contents of the universe can be imagined, a superbly long time ago to us, tightly clustered, arranged and compacted into one single body or mass, perhaps so much as such to be considered a solid, but now it is in the process of a phase change on the largest scale. The constant expansion of the universe is thought to be going at a faster rate now than previously hypothesized. From the solid to seemingly a gas, inasmuch as the solar systems and galaxies are separating in similar fashion to the way that atomic particles and molecular compounds would in a similarly vacuous space, like ice or water into steam. The catalyst or catalysts of this change of phase are debated over constantly, with theories ranging from the beatific to the happenstance. But whether it was God or random un-aided chemical interactions is irrelevant to the discussion at hand.

The second law of thermodynamics discusses the phenomena of increased entropy, or degree of disorder, of systems over time. As in, the more time passes, the more disordered a system will become. So, unhindered by time, how disordered will this system become? Into how small of increments are the contents of the universe breaking? That could depend on the size of the universe. If the true universe is actually smaller than the observable universe, and what looks to be more galaxies farther away are in fact just the reflected lights of closer galaxies that have traveled around the universe, then perhaps there is not much further to expand and disassemble. On the other hand, if the true universe is much larger then the observable universe, even potentially infinitely, then the potential for all of the galaxies to drift further from each other in all directions increases infinitely as well. Once the "great walls" of galaxies have separated into superclusters, the superclusters into clusters, and the clusters into galaxies, then the galaxies will have room to separate adequately from each other, room to expand themselves increases, which results in the drifting apart of the solar systems.

The Cosmological Principle, that is, the assumptions that the universe is homogeneous and that it is isotropic (basically the same uniformity in all directions,) supports the theory that the contents of the universe are acting like some supra-galactic-scale gas molecules. As the solar systems become increasingly separated from one another, this leaves space to be filled by the planets themselves. Thus the solar systems themselves begin to expand, each planet's orbit becoming larger and larger until one at a time they are lost by the gravitational pull of their sun and they fly off unhindered into space. The loss of energy created by the orbiting planets would lead to suns eventually burning themselves out and/or dissipating into nothingness, leaving the universe very cold and energy-less. Perhaps this would be the point at which a form of reciprocating universe theory might pertain, for if the contents of the universe used all of their energies expanding, once expanded what is there to do but condense. Condensation also being a resultant factor of cooling, it would then also follow the same theory: as the overall temperature of the universe decreased with each dying sun, then the contents of the universe would likely begin forming "solids" again, contracting and condensing, piece by piece in opposite order from which they separated via expansion.

The dead, lifeless planets (for there could be no life without the access to sun-energy) would collect with other planets and space debris, continuously until all mater was a disorganized soup, constantly condensing. As the condensing continued and the ambient temperature of space fell even further, the particles we call planets could begin to arrange themselves in an organized fashion, as do the particles of water in the phase change from steam to liquid to ice. The controls that make this seemingly impossible task actually functional at the atomic level are the same controls that make it work at the cosmic level: magnetic forces. One of the primary overall determinate mechanisms in existence, the positive attractive forces and negative repulsive forces of magnetism, work seemingly at odds and yet together they create the greatest order in known reality. They do this at the atomic particle level just the same as they do at the cosmic level, as is seemingly true with all of the mechanisms of existence: the universal laws of order work the same consistently throughout all existence regardless of size or place in the universe.

Thus it does not seem too far of a stretch of the imagination to suppose that planet Earth is but a veritable electron in this microcosm we call the universe. That, potentially, life extends infinitely in magnitude both directions, smaller and smaller infinitely, and larger and larger infinitely, so that our universe is perhaps just a simple cell in some larger organism, or perhaps just a mess of elements swirling around in a drop of water, and likewise, perhaps there is as much unseen activity on an electron as there is on Earth, who's residents and activities are also unseen from space. Perhaps, unbeknownst to us, we as humans are simply some form of bacterial organism or parasite or mechanism, and our larger position in the universe results in the ultimate destruction of whatever planet/galaxy/universe we inhabit by the total depletion of its resources and catastrophic disturbance of its natural cycles, simply a destructive mechanism in the universal law of entropy.

And now that we hypothesize that the planet Kepler-22b can support life, we can begin the quest to spread this disease– er.. thermodynamic mechanism– called humanity, and the disassembly of yet another solar-system.

Wow, we're good at this entropy thing!

about the author

Peter Karam is an artist and writer, living in a shack overlooking the sea, with his offspring, their part-fox -part-Nova-Scotia-Duck-Tolling-Retriever, and two chaotically-inclined twin-brother tuxedo-cats.

The essays in this edition were all written between 2009 and 2013.

find more from Port Townsend Publishing at
www.porttownsendpublishing.com